M.O.N.E.Y. MATRIX PRESENTS

PARABLES
FOR
PROFIT

VOL. 3

FACTS TELL—STORIES SELL

WOODY WOODWARD

© 2017 D.U. Publishing All Rights Reserved

Reproduction or translation of any part of this book beyond that permitted by Section 107 or 108 of the 1976 United States Copyright Act without written permission of the copyright owner is unlawful. Criminal copyright infringement is investigated by the FBI and may constitute a felony with a maximum penalty of up to five years in prison and/or a $250,000 fine. Request for permission or further information should be addressed to the Inspirational Product Division, D.U. Publishing.

>   D.U. Publishing
>   www.dupublishing.com

Warning—Disclaimer

The purpose of this book is to educate and inspire. This book is not intended to give advice or make promises or guarantees that anyone following the ideas, tips, suggestions, techniques or strategies will have the same results as the people listed throughout the stories contained herein. The author, publisher and distributor(s) shall have neither liability nor responsibility to anyone with respect to any loss or damage caused, or alleged to be caused, directly or indirectly by the information contained in this book.

ISBN: 978-0-9982340-5-2

M.O.N.E.Y. Matrix™ is registered trademark of Woody Woodward.

Contents

Introduction iii

What Price Would You Put On Your Dreams? 3

Do Your Sales Need Some CPR? 7

This Guy Lost $25 Million Making One Mistake,
Are You Doing The Same Thing? 11

What Is Your Time Worth? 15

What Drives You To Succeed? 20

Do You Know Who You Really Are? 27

What Opportunity Do You Need to Succeed? 32

This One Rule Will Change How You
Network Forever 36

What Is Your Why For What You Do? 39

This One Technique Will Create A Massive
Following For Your Business 45

When Was the Last Time
You Really Had Fun? 51

What Is The One Thing You Are Asking For
In Your Business? 53

Do You Have The Necessary
Leadership Skills To Win? 57

This One Technique
Can Save Your Company 61

Do Some Disadvantages Come With
A Hidden Upside?... 64

Decisions Determine Your Destiny—What Decisions
Do You Need To Make? 71

What Is Your Opportunity Worth?.. 75

Are You a Wrecker or Builder?.. 79

This One Technique Will Strengthen
Your Business 83

What Labels Are Holding You Back? 87

Introduction

Stories have a way of impacting our emotions. They help us make decisions, feel inspired to take action, or to become a better person. Before the written word, stories were passed down from generation to generation as an oral history. Today stories, parables, analogies help us convey or sell our message to others.

Parables for Profit is an 18-volume series with twenty stories per book to help you move an audience, motivate your teams and to increase your sells. Each series is patterned after the acronym of our M.O.N.E.Y. Matrix™ training modules. The acronym is as follows: M–Mindset, O–Opportunity, N–Networking, E–Entrepreneurship, Y–You (how to better yourself). At the end of each story there is a Call To Action. This is designed to help you build your business or if you are a manager to help your teams increase their revenue.

Each of these stories have been turned into videos that you can access at www.GetMoneyMatrix.com.

— M.O.N.E.Y. —

M.O.N.E.Y.

MINDSET

What Price Would You Put On Your Dreams?

A young man walked the lonely halls of his high school; he had just found out that his parents were selling their home. Life at the age of fifteen was pretty hard already, his mother lay in bed clinically depressed while his father tried to provide and hold the family together. Sadly, his dad lost his job and times were downright miserable. The entire family found work at the Titan Wheels factory as janitors and security patrol, each working eight hour shifts, even on school days. Things seemed to stabilize until his father had an argument with the factory manager. As a result, the entire family lost their jobs and lived out of their Volkswagen bus, bouncing around from one campground to another, finally settling at their aunt's house.

Always having a fond desire to make people laugh, this young man auditioned at Yuk Yuk's, a local comedy club, on an open mic night. Though his heart raced and his palms were sweaty, Jim Carrey broke through his fear and took the stage, dressed in a yellow polyester suit with tails, made by his mom.

His performance was a disaster.

But Jim wasn't ready to concede. He resolved to overcome this setback and make it as a comedian, no matter what. He spent the next two years refining his act, and after much work, time, and effort, returned to the stage. He became a local hit.

Carrey would not compromise his desire to make it in show business, and so he dropped out

MINDSET

of high school and moved to Los Angeles. He drove into Hollywood in his old Toyota with no work nor any prospects. He celebrated by writing himself a post-dated check for $10 million, keeping it with him as a source of inspiration. After being in the City of Angels for some time, he started picking up gigs at the world-famous Comedy Store. Then finally he got his big break, or so he thought. He was asked to perform on the Tonight Show with Johnny Carson. Mr. Carson had a tradition; if he thought a comedian was funny, he'd invite them to sit on his couch. For most comedians, this was a career changer. With his heart pounding in his chest, Carrey performed his routine. He looked to his right and caught a glimpse of Johnny giving him an "okay" sign but no invitation to the couch. He felt devastated.

Most people would have given up on their dream at this point. What reason did he have to hang onto hope? Over the next couple of years, Carrey earned many gigs and acting roles, but he had yet to make it big. Then, just three days before his father's death, Carrey received $10 million for the film The Mask. His dream had finally come true, only to be made bittersweet by the death of his father. At the funeral, Carrey slipped the old check that he had written to himself back when he lived in his beaten up Toyota into his dad's pocket before the coffin was closed.

Libraries and bookshelves in every town are filled with biographies of men and women who overcame their fear, beat unbeatable odds, and pressed through tragedy and heartache to get to the other side. Their stories demonstrate that beyond the fear lies blissful happiness and success.

Call to Action: Mindset

Today: How much do you want to make in you business in the next 365 days? Write yourself a post-dated check for one year from today for that amount, and carry it with you. To be safe, on the back of the check please write VOID so in case you lose it no one can cash it. If you will do this you will have a constant reminder to stay committed goals.

OPPORTUNITY

Do Your Sales Need Some CPR?

Whenever you go to any doctor, of any kind, for any condition, they will follow the three-part sequence of Examination, Diagnosis, and Prescription. In the sales world it is the same process. We meet with potential customers, examine their needs, diagnose their problems, and then prescribe a solution. Or do we? Sadly, I think most salespeople are like drug pushers. They meet a potential client, and they just push their drug no matter what, regardless if their drug will give the remedy their customer needs.

Every company needs some CPR. Think of salespeople as "Doctors of Sales," their products, services, or messages are providing needed air to their customers and businesses. When following the CPR of Sales, you begin to see significant results.

The CPR of Sales

C – Consulting (Examination Phase)

This is the examination phase where you need to ask questions specific to your customer's needs. Don't be a drug dealer pushing your products onto others. Ask questions so you know how to have your products solve their problems. If a doctor put your arm in a cast and your arm was not broken, you would never talk to that doctor again.

P – Personalize (Diagnostic Phase)

When you are diagnosing someone's situation, the

OPPORTUNITY

worst thing you can do is make it generic. People do not care how much you know until they know how much you care. Make the diagnosis all about them and how your expertise and knowledge can assist them. Even in the diagnosis phase, ask them additional questions to make sure you understand their needs. If you went in to see a doctor for a headache, and they didn't ask additional questions and check your vitals, they might miss additional issues with your health. Asking additional questions will help you have everything you need to recommend a product or services that will best suit their needs.

R – Recommend (Prescribe)

Since you were listening and asking poignant questions, you know exactly how to change your boring memorized sales pitch into a custom engaging presentation.

Sales trainer extraordinaire Brian Tracy said, "Professionals who sell in the way that doctors treat patients find that their sales activities proceed far more smoothly and result in better sales in less time."

OPPORTUNITY

Call to Action: Opportunity

Today:

Practice CPR selling on your family or friends. DO NOT start immediately using this in selling. Practice it in regular conversations with people you know to see how comfortable it can become. After you have had a couple practice rounds, then start to implement it into your business. If you will do this activity you will increase your sales.

NETWORKING

This Guy Lost $25 Million Making One Mistake, Are You Doing The Same Thing?

On June 22, 2001, Universal Pictures released *The Fast and the Furious*. This $38 million movie went on to gross $206 million. As you can imagine, immediately Universal wanted to do a sequel. Surprisingly, not everyone wanted to make another movie. One of the early problems was that Vin

NETWORKING

Diesel reportedly demanded $30 million to reprise his role as Dominic Toretto. Next, Rob Cohen, the director, dropped out because he did not like the new script.

To make up for Vin Diesel's absence, Paul Walker's character would need to be paired up with a strong personality. There were two options: fast talking "Edwin," played by rapper/actor Ja Rule, who was in the first movie, or create a new character, a never-before-seen childhood friend of Walker's played by actor Tyrese Gibson. This would be the first starring role for Ja Rule. The expanded role would also come with a massive paycheck. After earning just $15,000 for The Fast and the Furious, Ja Rule would earn $500,000 for the sequel. Furthermore, as one of the stars, Ja would be locked in to appear in all future movies with an ever-expanding paycheck.

At the time, Ja Rule's career was on fire. His 1999 debut album sold 3.6 million copies. His 2000 sophomore album sold 7.4 million copies. In 2001, his third album sold 9.6 million copies.

―――――― NETWORKING ――――――

His music label Murder Inc. was minting money and churning out hit after hit. Ja got too big for himself. He turned it down. He turned down a half a million dollars. New director John Singleton still needed to fill the role of a fast-talking street racer, so he turned to rapper Ludacris.

How'd This Turn Out For Tyrese Gibson and Ludacris?

After helping *2 Fast 2 Furious* earn $236 million at the box office, Gibson and Luda became an integral part of the Furious franchise. They have appeared in every sequel since. In total, the subsequent Furious movies earned $3.5 billion at the box office. Gibson and Luda earned $750,000 and $250,000 respectively to be in 2F2F, but they went on to earn $3-4 million for each sequel. Both men have a net worth that exceeds $25 million.

How'd This Turn Out For Ja Rule?

Unfortunately, 2001 turned out to be the absolute peak of Ja Rule's career. Remember how his 2001 album sold 9.6 million copies? His 2002 album sold just 1.5 million worldwide. His 2003 album sold just 468,000 copies. His net worth has dwindled by 80 percent.

Moral of the story: In business and life, check your ego at the door. Your net worth is equal to your network. When we walk around with inflatable egos, it destroys relationships and kills business opportunities.

Call to Action: Networking

Today:

Take the next fifteen minutes and journal about the top five people who have had a positive impact on your career. What skills did they have that made them successful? What are their top characteristics you would like to emulate in your business? If you will do this activity it will increase your network which will increase your net worth.

ENTREPRENEURSHIP

What Is Your Time Worth?

As an entrepreneur, one of the most important assets you have is your time. You cannot buy more, and you cannot replace it when it is lost. Here are a few techniques elite entrepreneurs use to optimize their time. If you implement these in your business you will be able to focus on what matters most.

Phone

- When you're busy, turn your phones to silent.
- Use voice-mail wisely and set aside times to return missed calls.
- Schedule times in the day when you will receive calls—let others know your schedule.

Email

- Only check your emails a couple of times a day. Close your email when it is not being used. New emails flashing up on your computer screen can be a huge distraction and time waster.
- Set up folders and rules in your email that help to automatically filter and file email messages.
- Schedule a block of time each day for sending and responding to emails. Don't let emails build up to unmanageable levels.

Mail

- Open your mail near a waste-paper basket and throw away unneeded items immediately.

- Deal with mail immediately if possible: read, process, and reply. Aim to handle each piece of mail only once.

Computers

- Turn off any instant messaging applications.

- Close programs and documents when you have finished using them—file your documents in a logical way. This not only removes distractions, but also means your computer has more resources for doing the next job.

- Close web pages after you have finished reading them. This is especially important for news or social networking sites where information is updated constantly.

Arranged Meetings

- Only attend meetings that are relevant to you. Is the meeting necessary and does it have a specific purpose?

- Aim to arrive on time for meetings, neither early nor late.

- Know the purpose of the meeting and get a copy of the agenda in advance. Arrange to leave the meeting early if it is only partially relevant.

- Agree in advance how long meetings will run. Start and end the meeting on time.
- Use a timed agenda, especially for longer meetings or where the chairperson is less effective.

Visitors—Impromptu Meetings

- Let people know when you are available to meet with visitors.
- Schedule blocks of time when you can meet with visitors and refer to these as appointments—try to limit each appointment to ten or fifteen minutes. The word appointment is more formal and people are less likely to think they are 'popping in for a chat' and more likely to come for a specific reason.
- Learn to say no. If visitors arrive at an inconvenient time, then politely explain that you cannot see them and schedule the visit for a mutually convenient time.

Call to Action: Entrepreneur

Today:

Chose only one of the activities from above and implement it immediately into your day. As soon as you have mastered one then add another. If you will do this activity you will be more productive and profitable.

YOU

What Drives You To Succeed?

While at a speaking engagement, Super Bowl Champion Joe Montana shared the following story about Jerry Rice:

During the summer training, this new rookie wide receiver comes onto the field, and on the first play catches the ball and sprints to the end zone. All he was supposed to do was catch the ball, run ten yards, and come back. I thought he was just trying to show off and would get tired by the end of the day. Well, one day turned into one week, and then three weeks. By the end of the month, every wide receiver caught his vision and would run the entire field to the end zone. I asked him why he did it, and he said, 'If I get that ball I am taking it to the end zone no matter what.'

The enthusiasm that burned within Jerry Rice became very contagious. His striving for excellence inspired his teammates to raise their standard of play. While with the 49ers, he was an integral part of their three Super Bowl Championship wins. He holds almost every record possible for someone in his position. Even if you are not a football fan, his accomplishments, compared to those who came in second, are astounding. His 1,549 receptions were 447 receptions ahead of the second place record held by Marvin Harrison. His 22,895 receiving yards were 7,961 yards ahead of the second place spot held by Tim Brown. His 197 touchdown receptions are 65 scores more than the 132 touchdown receptions by his former 49ers teammate Terrell Owens. And his 208 total touchdowns were 33 scores ahead of Emmitt Smith's second place 175.

Rice is remembered for his work ethic, enthusiasm, and dedication to the game. On August 24, 2006, he officially retired as a 49er, signing a one-day contract for $1,985,806.49. The number represented the year Rice was drafted (1985), his number (80), the year he retired (2006), and the 49ers (49). The figure was ceremonial, and Rice received no money, but he did enjoy a halftime ceremony to honor him during the 49ers' matchup with the Seattle Seahawks on November 19, 2006.

Here's another person who broke all the records. Charles Schwab was the first person to ever be paid a million dollar salary when annual salaries were around $5000. Why was Schwab paid 200 times the average wage earner? Was he 200 times smarter than the next guy? No. Did he work 200 times better than the next guy? Absurd. So what convinced Andrew Carnegie to pay Schwab such an exorbitant amount? It was Schwab's ability to arouse enthusiasm in his workers. He said, "A man can succeed at almost anything for which he has unlimited enthusiasm."

Call to Action: You

Today:

Take the next nine minutes and write down five things you are enthusiastic about in your business. Is it the lifestyle, the impact you are making, or the freedom you have? After you have identified your love for your business, share it on social media. You will find your enthusiasm is contagious which will lead to additional customers.

M.O.N.E.Y.

| M.O.N.E.Y. |

2

M.O.N.E.Y.

MINDSET

Do You Know Who You Really Are?

A seminary professor was vacationing with his wife in Gatlinburg, Tennessee. One morning, they were eating breakfast at a little restaurant, hoping to enjoy a quiet, family meal. While they were waiting for their food, they noticed a distinguished looking, white-haired man moving from table to table, visiting with the guests. The professor leaned over

―――――――――― | MINDSET | ――――――――――

and whispered to his wife, 'I hope he doesn't come over here.' But sure enough, the man did come over to their table.

'Where are you folks from?' he asked in a friendly voice.

'Oklahoma,' they answered.

'Great to have you here in Tennessee,' the stranger said. 'What do you do for a living?'

'I teach at a seminary,' he replied.

'Oh, so you teach preachers how to preach, do you? Well, I've got a really great story for you.' And with that, the gentleman pulled up a chair and sat down at the table with the couple. The professor groaned and thought to himself, 'Great... Just what I need... another preacher story!'

The man started, 'See that mountain over there?' (pointing out the restaurant window). 'Not far from the base of that mountain, there was a boy born to an unwed mother. He had a hard time growing up, because every place he went, he was always asked the same question, 'Hey boy, who's your daddy?' Whether he was at school, in the grocery store or

MINDSET

drug store, people would ask the same question, 'Who's your daddy?'

He would hide at recess and lunch time from other students. He would avoid going into stores because that question hurt him so bad. 'When he was about twelve-years old, a new preacher came to his church. He would always go in late and slip out early to avoid hearing the question, 'Who's your daddy?' But one day, the new preacher said the benediction so fast that he got caught and had to walk out with the crowd.

Just about the time he got to the back door, the new preacher, not knowing anything about him, put his hand on his shoulder and asked him, 'Son, who's your daddy?' The whole church got deathly quiet. He could feel every eye in the church looking at him. Now everyone would finally know the answer to the question, 'Who's your daddy?'

This new preacher, though, sensed the situation around him and using discernment that only the Holy Spirit could give, said the following to that scared little boy, 'Wait a minute! I know who you are! I see the family resemblance now, You Are a Child of God.'

With that he patted the boy on his shoulder and said, 'Boy, you've got a great inheritance. Go and claim it.' With that, the boy smiled for the first time in a long time and walked out the door a changed person. He was never the same again. Whenever anybody asked him, 'Who's your Daddy?' he'd just tell them, 'I'm a Child of God.''

The distinguished gentleman got up from the table and said, 'Isn't that a great story?'

The professor responded that it really was a great story!

As the man turned to leave, he said, 'You know, if that new preacher hadn't told me that I was one of God's children, I probably never would have amounted to anything!' And he walked away.

The seminary professor and his wife were stunned. He called the waitress over and asked her, 'Do you know who that man was, the one who just left that was sitting at our table?'

The waitress grinned and said, 'Of course. Everybody here knows him. That's Ben Hooper.

MINDSET

He's governor of Tennessee!'

When Ben Hooper saw himself through a different perspective he acted accordingly and changed his life forever. Our mindset influences our outcomes. How do you see yourself? Are you holding on to negative images from your childhood? Or do you see yourself as someone who deserves to succeed? Your mindset will have a direct impact on the actions you take. Your actions dictate your results. The old adage from Henry Ford is still true today: "Whether you think you can or you think you can't, you are right."

Call to Action: Mindset

Today:

Be hyper sensitive to what you think about yourself and others. Go twenty-four hours without pondering on a negative attribute about yourself or someone else. If you find yourself having negative thoughts, repeat the mantra—I am who I am, I will be who I will be, therefore today I am free.

OPPORTUNITY

What Opportunity Do You Need to Succeed?

Have you heard of Louis Delgado or Skipper Mullins? In early 1968, Chuck Norris suffered the tenth and last loss of his career, losing an upset decision to Louis Delgado. On November 24, 1968, he avenged his defeat to Delgado, and by doing so, won the Professional Middleweight Karate champion title, which he held for six consecutive years. In 1969, he

OPPORTUNITY

won Karate's triple crown for the most tournament wins of the year and the Fighter of the Year award by Black Belt Magazine. Delgado and Mullins were world champions as well and at times in their career beat Norris, but why is it that most people have not heard of them? It comes down to opportunities.

While at a sparing tournament in Long Beach, California, Norris met martial arts master Bruce Lee. They became fast friends because of their love of martial arts. In 1968, Lee and Norris started talking about working together. While Lee was the stunt coordinator for the film Wrecking Crew, starring Dean Martin, he gave Norris his first acting job. Norris's part was a fight scene with Martin, preceded by one line of dialogue!

In 1972, Bruce was directing Return of the Dragon and wanted the world champion Norris to be his opponent. Bruce said with excitement, "We'll have a fight in the Coliseum in Rome, two gladiators in a fight to the death! Best of all, we can choreograph it ourselves. I promise you the fight will be the highlight of the film."

OPPORTUNITY

"Great," said Norris, "Who wins?"

"I do," said Bruce with a laugh. "I'm the star!"

"Oh, you're going to beat up on the current world karate champion?"

"No," said Bruce. "I'm going to kill the current world karate champion."

Norris laughed and agreed to do the movie, after gaining twenty pounds at Lee's request

What would have happened to Chuck Norris if he was not given this opportunity as an actor? Most likely he would have retired from martial arts and opened up his own gym in his home town as did other previous champions. What would have happened to Bruce Lee if it wasn't for fighting the world champion in the historic coliseum? Most likely, Return of the Dragon would be clumped together with other martial arts films that never went anywhere. Instead, by creating an opportunity for both of them to showcase their talents, the two individuals were stronger together than apart. Due to their combined efforts, Return of the Dragon has been voted by critics and consumers as the greatest martial arts film of all time.

Call to Action: Opportunity

Today:

Take the next twelve minutes and identify who would be your Chuck Norris. Who would be your ideal joint venture partner? Reach out to them and start talking to them about teaming up on a project that will build both of your careers. If you will do this activity you too will expand your brand and business like Bruce Lee and Chuck Norris.

NETWORKING

This One Rule Will Change How You Network Forever

There are four rules of communication. Each rule has a different level of how to conduct yourself in networking.

Rule #1 – The Pewter Rule:
"Do unto them before they do it to you." This is

the lowest of the rules. The Pewter Rule is the epitome of being selfish. It means I am going to hurt someone before they can hurt me, this way I am protecting myself. It never works. If we are trying to protect ourselves by hurting others first, we will never create a profitable network.

Rule #2 – The Silver Rule:

"Do unto yourself as you would want others to do unto you." This rule is quite selfish, and we see it far too often. It means I am going to take what I want before someone takes if from me. Yes, it is great to do things for yourself, but the Silver Rule means you are only going to take care of yourself and ignore others. This will only alienate you and drive a wedge between you and everyone else.

Rule #3 – The Golden Rule:

"Do unto others as you would want them to do unto you." The Golden Rule that most people live by is good but not great. It too is selfish. It says, "I am going to treat you the way I want to be treated."

Maybe I don't want to be treated that same way you want to be treated.

Rule #4 – The Platinum Rule:

"Do unto others as they would want you to do unto them."

Dr. Tony Alessandra has coined the phrase, "The Platinum Rule." To me, this rule is doing unto others based off of the way they want to be done unto. Find out what drives your friends, family, and customers, and treat them accordingly.

Call to Action: Networking

Today:

Take the next nine minutes and call your favorite customer. Ask them how you can best serve them. You may find other customers want to be treated the same way. If you will do this activity you will create a referring network of customers.

ENTREPRENEURSHIP

What Is Your Why For What You Do?

Speaker, author Simon Sinek has a compelling reason for understanding your *Why*:

"I call it the Golden Circle:
Why (in the center)
How (in the middle ring)
What (the outside ring)"

ENTREPRENEURSHIP

This little idea explains why some organizations and some leaders are able to inspire where others aren't. Let me define the terms really quickly: Every single person, every single organization on the planet knows what they do—100 percent. Some know how they do it, whether you call it your differentiated value proposition or your proprietary process or your USP. But very very few people or organizations know why they do what they do.

By why I don't mean to make a profit—that's a result. It's always a result. By why I mean, what's your purpose? What's your cause? What's your belief? Why does your organization exist? Why do you get out of bed in the morning? And why should anyone care? As a result the way we think, the way we act, the way we communicate, is from the outside in– (from What to Why). It's obvious. We go from the clearest thing to the fuzziest thing. But the inspired leaders, and the inspired organizations, regardless of their size, regardless of their industry, all think, act, and communicate from the inside out (from Why to How).

ENTREPRENEURSHIP

Let me give you an example: I use Apple because they are easy to understand and everybody gets it. If Apple were like everyone else, a marketing message from them might sound like this: "We make great computers. They are beautifully designed, simple to use, and user friendly—Wanna buy one?" That's how most of us communicate. That's how most marketing is done. That's how most sales are done, and that is how most of us communicate interpersonally. We say what we do, we say how we are different or better, and we expect some sort of behavior, a purchase or a vote, something like that. Like "Here is our new law firm, we have the best lawyers with the biggest clients, always perform for our clients, do business with us" or " Here is our new car, it gets great gas mileage, it has leather seats, buy our car." But it's uninspiring.

Here is how Apple actually communicates: "In everything we do we believe in challenging the status quo, we believe in thinking differently. The way we challenge the status quo is by making our products beautifully designed, simple to use, and user friendly. We just happen to make great computers—wanna buy one?" Totally different. Right? You are ready to buy a computer from me. All I did was reverse the order of the information.

What it proves to us is that people don't buy what you do, they buy why you do it. Again, people do not buy what you do, they buy why you do it. This explains why every single person is perfectly comfortable buying a computer from Apple. But we are also perfectly comfortable buying an MP3 player from Apple, or a phone from Apple, or a DVR from Apple. But as I said before, Apple is just a computer company. There is nothing that distinguishes them structurally from any of their competitors; their competitors are all equally qualified to make all of these products. In fact, they tried.

A few years ago, Gateway came out with flat screen tvs. They are eminently qualified to make flat screen tvs; they have been making flat screen monitors for years. Nobody bought one. Dell came out with MP3 players and PDAs, and they make great quality products and they can make perfectly well-designed products. Nobody bought one. In fact, in talking about it now, we can't even imagine buying an MP3 player from Dell—why would you buy an MP3 player from a computer company? But we do it every day.

People don't buy what you do they buy why you do it. When we communicate from the outside in (from How to Why), yes people can understand vast amounts of complicated information like features and benefits and facts and figures. It just doesn't drive behavior. When we communicate from the inside out (from Why to How), we are talking directly to that part of the brain that controls behavior. And we then allow people to rationalize it with the tangible things we say and do—this is where 'gut decisions' come from. Sometime you can give somebody all the facts and figures and they say, 'I know what all the facts and details say, but it just doesn't feel right." Why would we use that verb? It doesn't feel right?

Because the part of the brain that controls decision making doesn't control language. And the

ENTREPRENEURSHIP

best we can muster up is 'I don't know, it just doesn't feel right." Or sometimes you say you are leading with your heart or leading with your soul; I hate to break it to you, but those aren't other body parts controlling your behavior. It's all happening in your in your limbic brain, the part of your brain that controls decision making and not language.

But if YOU don't know why you do what you do, and people respond to why you do what you do, then how will you ever get people to vote for you or buy something from you or more importantly be loyal?

Call to Action: Entrepreneurship

Today:

Take the next ten minute and identify your Why. What drives you to get out of bed each morning? Why do you build your organization? What is your driving force? If you will do this activity you will have clarity to your purpose which will translate to your message with your customers.

YOU

This One Technique Will Create A Massive Following For Your Business

On June 30, 1859, Jean Francois Gravelot, better known as the Great Blondin, became the first person to cross Niagara Falls on a tight rope. It was a death defying act, 160 feet above the river. That year he would do it eight different times. Each

YOU

time the crowds would grow larger and larger.

One time, in front of 25,000 people, he asked the audience if they believed he could cross the tight rope using stilts. They all shouted, "We believe, we believe!" He proceeded to cross using just stilts. Another time he asked the audience if they believed he could balance a chair on the tight rope and sit atop the chair. They shouted, "We believe, we believe!" And so he did.

A few months later, he asked if they believed he could push a wheelbarrow across and again they erupted, "We believe, we believe!" He then pushed the wheelbarrow across and asked, "Who believes I can put a person in the wheelbarrow and push them across?" The crowd of 100,000 exploded in cheers chanting, "We believe, we believe!" Then the Great Blondin said, "Which one of you will get in the wheelbarrow?" The crowd went silent.

His manager, Harry Colcord, said he would let the Great Blondin carry him on his back across the tight rope. On August 14th, in front of a hundred thousand people, Harry crossed Niagara Falls on

YOU

Blondin's back. The newspapers on the other side asked Colcord why he would do such a thing. He was not under contract; there was no obligation for him to do so. He replied, "I have watched his discipline, I know his work ethic and his commitment to his craft. I knew he would not drop me."

The secret to success is following business fundamentals until those fundamentals turn into your routine and your routine creates your habits.

Call to Action: You

Today:

Take fifteen minutes and review your daily routine and ask yourself, "Are my actions based on true successful fundamentals?" If they are not, look for the proper fundamentals that will produce the habits you want to have. If you will do this activity you will build leadership characteristics like Blondin where other people will follow you.

M.O.N.E.Y.

— | M.O.N.E.Y. | —

3

M.O.N.E.Y.

MINDSET

**When Was the Last Time
You Really Had Fun?**

How often do you see a three-year old on anti-depressants? Never! And it's not because pharmaceutical companies don't want to get a new batch of customers. The reason why young kids don't need them is because they are always playing. Dr. Stuart Brown, the founder of the National Institute of Play, said, "The opposite of Play is not Work it

MINDSET

is Depression." Science has found four top benefits for adults who play: It relieves stress, improves brain function, stimulates the mind and boosts creativity, and improves relationships and connections to others.

As entrepreneurs, we get so stressed because of our demanding careers. Ask yourself, when was the last time you really played? When was the last time you really had fun? When was the last time you really laughed out loud?

Call to action: Mindset

Today:

Take the next nine minutes and find a funny video on YouTube and share it with friend or post it on social media. By doing this activity you will also remind other people about the importance of play.

OPPORTUNITY

**What Is The One Thing
You Are Asking For
In Your Business?**

When my friend Woody Woodward was filming his first movie (i-ology), he needed over 250 clips of High Definition (HD) stock footage. The average price per clip was about $900. After researching the best company in the industry, he called the secretary and asked for the person in charge of

———————| OPPORTUNITY |———————

stock footage. Upon getting her name, he called 1-800-FLOWERS and sent her a basket of flowers with a note that said, "Thank you in advance for helping me with my movie project. Sincerely, Woody Woodward (951) XXX-XXXX." He received a phone call within three days from this woman saying, "Who are you and why do I have flowers on my desk?"

Woody went on to tell her how he needed her company to donate stock footage for his movie. She instructed him that it was impossible; the company did not donate footage. Focusing on how "You Get 100 percent of What You Don't Ask For," he remained persistent. Woody continued to persevere, and she said she would talk to her boss. She said if he listed every clip he would need, she would revisit the idea in thirty days. After he hung up, he called the secretary again and asked for the name of her boss and sent the boss flowers and chocolates with a note stating the same thing. Over the next thirty days, he sent two more packages, one with movie passes and candy saying, "Enjoy a movie on me." At the end of the thirty days, he did not get the footage for free, instead they were willing to support him with as many clips as he needed for only $50.00 a clip.

In business there are two types of R.O.I. The most commonly known is Return On Investment. What Woody used was a Return On Importance. Dr. David Schwartz said, "Man's most compelling non-biological hunger is to feel important." When we make others feel important, it changes the way we do business. Not only does it have value socially, but monetarily as well. Woody's investment to make them feel important cost him about $257.83 for the packages sent. His return on making them feel important, however, was about $200,000.

You get 100 percent of what you don't ask for. If you ask for nothing, you get 100 percent of nothing. One of the top fundamentals we need to master in business is the Power of the Ask, while at the same time making the other person feel important.

OPPORTUNITY

Call to Action: Opportunity

Today: Go ask for something crazy! When you are out, ask for the free upgrade, call that one potential client you have been afraid to talk to and make the "ask," go out on a limb and ask for something ridiculous that will prosper your business.

―――――― NETWORKING ――――――

Do You Have
The Necessary
Leadership Skills To Win?

Already a celebrated polar explorer, Sir Ernest Shackleton coordinated the British Imperial Trans-Antarctic Expedition with the goal of accomplishing the first crossing of the Antarctic continent, a feat he considered to be the last great polar journey of the "Heroic Age of Exploration."

NETWORKING

In December 1914, Shackleton set sail with his 27-man crew, many of whom had responded to the following recruitment ad: "Men wanted for hazardous journey. Small wages. Bitter cold. Long months of complete darkness. Constant danger. Safe return doubtful. Honor and recognition in case of success. —Ernest Shackleton."

Ice conditions were unusually harsh, and the wooden ship, that Shackleton had renamed Endurance after his family motto Fortitudine Vincimus ("by endurance we conquer"), became trapped in the pack ice of the Weddell Sea. For ten months, the Endurance drifted, locked within the ice, until the pressure crushed the ship. With meager food, clothing, and shelter, Shackleton and his men were stranded on the ice floes, where they camped for five months.

When they had drifted to the northern edge of the pack and encountered open water, the men sailed the three small lifeboats they'd salvaged to a bleak crag called Elephant Island. They were on land for the first time in 497 days; however, it was

NETWORKING

uninhabited and, due to its distance from shipping lanes, provided no hope for rescue.

Recognizing the severity of the physical and mental strains on his men, Shackleton and five others immediately set out to take the crew's rescue into their own hands. In a 22-foot lifeboat they accomplished the impossible, surviving a 17-day, 800-mile journey through the world's worst seas to South Georgia Island, where a whaling station was located.

The six men landed on a desolate part of the island. Their last hope was to cross 26 miles of mountains and glaciers, considered impassable, to reach the whaling station on the other side. Starved, frostbitten, and wearing rags, Shackleton and two others made the trek, and in August 1916, 21 months after the initial departure of the Endurance, Shackleton himself returned to rescue the men on Elephant Island. Although they'd withstood the most incredible hardship and privation, not one member of the 27-man crew was lost.

Ernest Shackleton is one of the greatest leaders

NETWORKING

who has ever lived. What made him so great? His willingness to put his men before his own selfish needs.

Call to Action: Networking

Today:

Take this time to reach out to your team, employees, and clients to find a way to serve them. Here are a few ideas you can do to serve those you work with:

- Write them a thank you note
- On social media, post something about their success not yours
- Recommend them for a promotion, job, or advancement
- Call or text them and let them know you were thinking about them

ENTREPRENEURSHIP

This One Technique Can Save Your Company

An elderly carpenter was ready to retire. He told his employer-contractor of his plans to leave the house-building business to live a more leisurely life with his wife and enjoy his extended family. He would miss the paycheck each week, but he wanted to retire. They could get by.

The contractor was sorry to see his good worker

ENTREPRENEURSHIP

go and asked if he could build just one more house as a personal favor. The carpenter said yes, but over time it was easy to see that his heart was not in his work. He resorted to shoddy workmanship and used inferior materials. It was an unfortunate way to end a dedicated career.

When the carpenter finished his work, his employer came to inspect the house. Then he handed the front-door key to the carpenter and said, "This is your house... my gift to you."

The carpenter was shocked! What a shame! If he had only known he was building his own house, he would have done it so differently.

So it is with us. We build our lives, a day at a time, often putting less than our best into the building. Then, with a shock, we realize we have to live in the house we have built. If we could do it over, we would do it differently.

But, you cannot go back. You are the carpenter, and every day you hammer a nail, place a board, or erect a wall. Someone once said, "Life is a do-it-yourself project." As an entrepreneur you are often called on to be many things from the CEO, to the receptionist, to the IT engineer, to the delivery person. Sometimes there is a desire to cut corners to save time. Remember, your attitude, and the choices you make today, help build the "house" you will live in tomorrow. Therefore, build wisely!

Call To Action—Entrepreneurship

Today:

Take the next ten minutes and truly strategize your day. Is there any work you do that can be subcontract out to help you be more productive? Is there a strategic partner you can create a joint venture with? If you will do this activity you will realize you are not alone. Create the team to stream your dream.

YOU

Do Some Disadvantages Come With A Hidden Upside?

Malcolm Gladwell, New York Times bestselling author of The Tipping Point, Blink and Outliers, thinks the answer is a resounding yes—some disadvantages do come with a hidden upside.

Gladwell calls this phenomenon "compensation learning." People who lack certain skills—for

YOU

dyslexics, the ability to read easily—make up for the weakness in other, often more important, areas.

As an example, Gladwell describes how the best dyslexic learners cope from a young age: If you can't complete your first-grade reading assignment, you get a friend to do it for you. That's delegating. When your teacher chides you for not turning in a paper, you talk your way out of the jam. That's communication. As you continue through school, you assemble a group of people who like you and are willing to help you out. That's leadership. And each time another hurdle comes your way, you problem-solve around it.

"So you take this group of people, this small group of successful compensators, and they emerge out of high school, or college if they get that far, and they want to start a business, and they have been practicing the four skills that are absolutely essential for entrepreneurship," Gladwell explains. "Delegation, leadership, oral communication, problem solving. They've taken a graduate level course in the four most important traits by virtue of the fact that life dealt them one of its most grievous disadvantages."

One person who did just this is Richard Branson. The now billionaire founder of the Virgin Group dropped out of school when he was sixteen after struggling in class and being called lazy by his teachers. But out in the real world, the skills that had previously held him back helped him flourish.

Richard Branson said, "My dyslexia guided the way we communicated with customers. When we launched a new company, I made sure that I was shown the ads and marketing materials.... If I could grasp it quickly, then we knew our customers would."

Roughly one in five people are thought to be affected by dyslexia, and Gladwell says some estimates say 33 percent of American entrepreneurs have it or a similar disability. Charles Schwab, Ted Turner, Tommy Hilfiger, Steven Spielberg, Thomas Edison, Walt Disney and William Hewitt are on a long list of business titans that credit their learning disabilities as a factor to their eventual success.

Call to Action: You

Today:

Take the next thirteen minutes and write down five things you used to be poor at doing but now have mastered. For example, "I used to be afraid of talking to people about my business but now I can talk to almost anyone" or "I used to have a difficult time presenting in front of the room but now I am pretty good at doing it." As you list these previous experiences you will realize whatever challenge you are currently going through will someday be a future strength.

MINDSET

——————— | MINDSET | ———————

SERIES

4

MINDSET

MINDSET

Decisions Determine Your Destiny— What Decisions Do You Need To Make?

The screaming and yelling wouldn't stop. This young couple were constantly fighting over money. They were so broke the husband had to sell his dog for $50 to buy food. During these dark days, he saw a fight between world heavyweight champion Muhammad

―――――――――― | MINDSET | ――――――――――

Ali and Chuck Wepner, an underdog whom no one thought would make it past the third round. Inspired by this match, he sat down and for the next 84 hours he wrote an inspirational movie script about an underdog.

Month after month he would present his script to movie producers but was constantly rejected. The financial burden continued to put a strain on his marriage. After being turned down countless times, he got a chance to sell the script for $75,000 on one condition—he was not going to be the actor. Even though he was broke and hungry, he impulsively stood his ground and declined the offer. The only way he was going to sell the script was if he was the lead actor. The company refused. Eventually, the production company offered him $250,000, and then they offered $1 million for the script with the same stipulation, he was not to be the actor. He said no to each offer. He was desperate but was not willing to sellout on his dream. They finally gave in and offered to do the movie on a shoestring budget, giving him

MINDSET

$35,000 as the writer and actor; if the movie was successful, he would share in the profits. He immediately agreed.

This young inexperienced actor was Sylvester Stallone and the movie he wrote was Rocky. He was not willing to back down from his dream to be an actor even though he was in a horrible financial situation. Your destiny is determined by the decisions you make when you are in your darkest hours. Stallone said, "Once in one's life, for one mortal moment, one must make a grab for immortality; if not, one has not lived."

As Rocky Balboa said:

"Let me tell you something you already know, the world ain't all sunshine and rainbows. It's a very mean and nasty place, and I don't care how tough you are it will beat you to your knees and keep you there permanently if you let it. You, me, or nobody is gonna hit as hard as life. But it ain't about how hard you hit, it's about how hard you can get hit

MINDSET

and keep moving forward. How much can you take and keep moving forward? That's how winning is done. Now if you know what your worth then go out and get what your worth, but you gotta be willing to take the hits and not pointing fingers saying you ain't where you wanna be because of him or her and anybody. Cowards do that, and that ain't you. You're better than that."

Call To Action: Mindset

Today:

Take the next twelve minutes and make a decision that will have a positive impact on your business. Is it to make that ONE call you know you need to make? Is it to get out there a do one more presentation? If you will do this activity you will control your destiny.

OPPORTUNITY

What Is Your Opportunity Worth?

In the 1990s and early 2000s, Blockbuster was everywhere. At its peak in 2004, Blockbuster had more than 60,000 employees in over 9,000 stores. Today, the company is out of business. Netflix, on the other hand is booming with more than 30 million subscribers and a market cap of $34 billion. But did you know that Blockbuster could have controlled both the mail order DVD and streaming business with a simple, relatively inexpensive

OPPORTUNITY

acquisition? Unfortunately, a fateful decision in 2000 set the company on the road to disaster.

In the spring of 2000, Netflix CEO Reed Hastings boarded a private plane and flew from San Jose to Dallas for a meeting with video rental giant Blockbuster. At the time, Blockbuster had 7,700 stores worldwide renting mainly VCR tapes.

Hastings had co-founded Netflix three years earlier. He was banking on a pair of then emerging technologies: DVDs and a website where movie watchers could order with a click of a mouse. For $20 a month, subscribers could rent an unlimited number of DVDs, one at a time. The DVDs arrived in the mail in the now iconic red envelopes.

Hastings, a Silicon Valley engineer, was convinced that eventually movies could be rented more conveniently (and cheaply) by streaming them over the Internet. However, technology was not quite there yet in 2000, and Netflix was losing money. The company had only 300,000 subscribers and they were relying on the U.S. Postal Service to get their movies to their customers.

OPPORTUNITY

So, seeking a lifeline, Hastings approached Blockbuster with an idea. He wanted Netflix to become Blockbuster's streaming service. He proposed that Blockbuster buy a 49 percent stake in Netflix and absorb the Blockbuster name. The price for that 49 percent stake? $50 million.

Blockbuster passed. Hastings wasn't one to take no for an answer. After getting rejected once, he went back to Blockbuster at least three more times to pitch the deal. Blockbuster declined every time. So Hastings flew back to California and went to work promoting Netflix. Four years later, Blockbuster launched its own subscription service, but by then, it was too late. Hastings has admitted that if Blockbuster had launched their own service even two years earlier, they would have driven Netflix out of business.

However, by 2005, Netflix had 4.2 million subscribers and that number was growing steadily. Meanwhile Blockbuster was on a downward spiral. Their subscription service was launched too late and could not find traction. By 2007 when Netflix began streaming movies and TV shows directly to computers, it had not just beat Blockbuster at its own game, but it entirely reinvented the game in the process.

The moral of the story is that the grass is not always greener somewhere else. Sometimes you just need to water and fertilize your own opportunities like Hastings did with Netflix.

Call to Action: Opportunity

Today:

Take fifteen minutes and get really clear on what your opportunity is and how you can better convey it to other people. If you will do this activity you will be far more agile and competitive.

NETWORKING

Are You a Wrecker or Builder?

I watched them tearing a building down,
  A gang of men in a busy town.
  With a ho-heave-ho and lusty yell,
  They swung a beam and a sidewall fell.
I asked the foreman, "Are these men skilled,
  As the men you'd hire if you had to build?"
  He gave me a laugh and said, "No indeed!

NETWORKING

> Just common labor is all I need.
>
> I can easily wreck in a day or two
> What builders have taken a year to do."
> And I thought to myself as I went my way,
> Which of these two roles have I tried to play?
>
> Am I a builder who works with care,
> Measuring life by the rule and square?
> Am I shaping my deeds by a well-made plan,
> Patiently doing the best I can?
>
> Or am I a wrecker who walks the town,
> Content with the labor of tearing down?

When it comes to networking, the most important thing you can do is build up your relationships instead of pulling them down. What are you doing to help other people be successful? Being an entrepreneur means you have unbelievable demands on your schedule; however, the old adage of "You can have everything in life you want, if you will just help enough other people get what they want" still rings true. When auto shop owner Claudio Zampolli took time out of his busy schedule to connect Eddy Van

NETWORKING

Halen to Sammy Hagar, it came back to him when the newly-formed Van Halen was selling out auditoriums worldwide. Where did Eddy and Sammy go to buy their cars? Claudio Zampolli.

Just when Theodore Geisel was about to give up as an author he ran into old college roommate Marshall McClintock who encouraged him to keep following his passion. McClintock that day was just made children's editor for Vanguard Press. Through networking together, Geisel published his first children's, *And To Think I Saw It On Mulberry Street*, under the pen name Dr. Seuss. Many years later when Dr. Seuss was at the height of his career, he started Beginner Books and was able to return the favor by publishing McClintock's first book.

As you help others build their businesses, they will in return help you build yours. We are all one relationship away from taking our businesses to the next level. If we don't have the necessary relationships we need, then we need to access them through other people's relationships, and that is at the core of networking.

NETWORKING

Call To Action: Networking

Today:

When you are meeting with potential clients or business associates, ask them what is the #1 business problem they need solved. When you get back to your office take fifteen minutes and research a solution for them and share with them what you found. As you solve other people's problems they will help you solve yours.

ENTREPRENEURSHIP

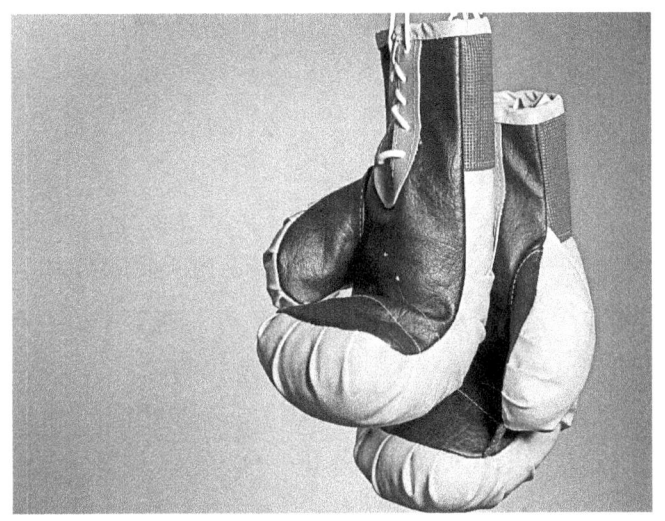

This One Technique Will Strengthen Your Business

Every year from 2009 to 2015, boxer Floyd Mayweather has been the highest paid athlete in the world. He earned around $105 million in 2014 alone. That was $25 million more than the second highest paid athlete. And perhaps what's most impressive is that Floyd earned $105 million

ENTREPRENEURSHIP

without a single meaningful endorsement deal. Floyd's rise to absolute financial dominance in the sports world never would have happened without one very simple decision back in 2006.

Between 1996 and 2006, Floyd was represented by Bob Arum's Top Rank Boxing promotional company. In boxing, when you are signed with a promoter, you are basically an employee. You are offered a set amount of money to appear at a fight. The promoter puts up all the money and takes on all the risks to organize the fight. By taking on the risk, the promoter also reaps the biggest rewards. Whatever profits were left over after costs were paid off (including the cost to pay the fighters), would go straight to Bob Arum's pockets. This is the Business Behind The Boxing Business.

Back in April 2006, Bob Arum offered Floyd $8 million to fight Antonio Margarito. It would have doubled Floyd's previous highest purse. Instead of accepting, Floyd countered by saying he wanted $20 million to fight Oscar De La Hoya. Arum was stunned. Arum also didn't think that amount of

ENTREPRENEURSHIP

money for Floyd to fight Oscar would pay off. So he declined and kept pushing the Margarito bout.

At this point, Floyd became an entrepreneur and learned the business behind the business.

The fight with De La Hoya took place in May 2007 with Mayweather taking home $25 million after paying all the costs. It became the highest revenue-producing fight in boxing history up to that point.

Today Floyd puts on every aspect of his own fights. That means he fronts all the money for an event, including his opponent's purse. When he fought Saul Alvarez in September 2013, Floyd cut him a $10 million check from his personal checking account weeks before the fight. Floyd also paid tens of millions of his own money for the event space, the vendors, the food, beverages, etc. That's the downside. The upside is that when the fight was over, Floyd got the lion's share of profits. In the Alvarez fight, Floyd walked away with $75 million.

The same math is basically true with the Manny Pacquiao fight. Floyd fronted most of the costs to

ENTREPRENEURSHIP

organize the event and cut Manny a $50 million guaranteed check to show up. When the night is over, Floyd will get 60 percent of the profits. Normally he would get 100 percent, but he had to make some concessions to get Manny to show up. But even with "just" 60 percent of the profit share, Floyd earned $200 million from this one fight alone.

When Mayweather was under Bob Arum his ten-year career earnings were $10 million. When he learned the business behind the business and opened Mayweather Promotions, his career earnings just in the last eight years ballooned to $610 Million.

Call To Action: Entrepreneurship

Today:

Take fifteen minutes and find out what is the business behind your business? Who is the top income earner in your industry? Research how they got to that spot. Discover what you need to do differently to multiply your income.

---- YOU ----

What Labels Are Holding You Back?

Back in the times of the "Old Wild West," two brothers were caught stealing saddles. As punishment for stealing, their hands were branded with the initials "ST" for Saddle Thief. One brother, disgraced by his actions, traveled the frontier from town to town trying to escape his guilt. Eventually he died penniless and was buried in an unmarked

YOU

grave. The other brother accepted his fate and decided change his behavior but stayed in the town where he had committed his crime. He spent his life earning back the respect of the townspeople.

Many years later a traveler who came through the town noticed the faded marks on the old timer's hands and inquired from the locals what it meant. One replied, "I don't know, but when my cattle broke my fence he was the first one to help me bring them back to pasture." Another replied, "When my little Johnny was lost he organized a search party and brought him home." One after another each local told a story of how this man had helped them. Finally, one local said, "I don't know what the initials originally meant, but I think the letters are the abbreviation for Saint."

Your past does not represent your future. No matter what mistakes you have made in your personal life, relationships, or business they do not have power over your future unless you let them.

Ursula Burns grew up in the Lower East Side of New York which was a hub for gangs. Burns

YOU

was raised by her single mother in a housing project. Her mother ran a daycare center out of her home and ironed shirts so that she could afford to send Ursula to Catholic school. She went to NYU and from there became an intern at Xerox. She's now Xerox's CEO and chairwoman. She's the first African-American woman to be the head of a Fortune 500 Company.

John Paul DeJoria had it rough from the beginning. His German and Italian parents divorced when he was two, and he sold Christmas cards and newspapers to help support his family before he turned ten. He was eventually sent to live in a foster home in Los Angeles. DeJoria spent some time as an L.A. gang member before joining the military. After trying his hand as an employee for Redken Laboratories, he took a $700 loan and created John Paul Mitchell Systems. He hawked the company's shampoo door-to-door, living out of his car while doing so. But the quality of the product could not be denied, and now the John Paul Mitchell Systems does a billion dollars annually.

---| YOU |---

In the early 1990s, J.K. Rowling had just gotten divorced and was living on welfare with her infant daughter. She completed most of the first Harry Potter book in cafes. Nothing in her past said she would become the author of one of the top-selling books and movie franchise of all time. The Harry Potter franchise has become a worldwide success, and J.K. Rowling is now worth an estimated $1 billion.

No matter what challenge you are currently facing, it does not hold you back from creating the future you want to have. You just need a plan.

Call to Action: You

Today:

Take the next thirteen minutes and plan your future. What is your big hairy audacious goal for your business? Write it down and post it on your next to your computer so you can see it every day. If you will do this activity you will have a clear picture for steering your company.

www.ingramcontent.com/pod-product-compliance
Lightning Source LLC
Chambersburg PA
CBHW052131010526
44113CB00034B/1806